Haiku
from the Home of
Reverend MoFo Jones

Also by Jeffrey Dessources

do not hold doors

Haiku
from the Home of
Reverend MoFo Jones

Jeffrey Dessources

grew bap books New York 2008

www.mrjeffdess.com

grew bap books

For all you true MoFo's out there

Contents

Motherfucker… it's about expression. Don't be ashamed of the word MoFo. Cus the word MoFo is a noun it describes a person,place or thing.

-Bernie Mac from the film *Kings of Comedy*

Note to the Reader

Centuries before I took my first breath Reverend MoFo Jones was known to roam various projects, barrios, town houses and galaxies, spreadin love, talking bout the home and fucking with people's heads. Responsible for all types of other miscellaneous mumbo jumbo the good Reverend should have been the biggest thing since the introduction of Stefan Urquelle, but this was not the case. Although the Reverend knew mad folks, not many if any were aware of the good Rev., which became an issue. The non existent PR team held a number of imaginary events that nobody attended. The Evites never went out, the bottles weren't getting popped, and there were no hype men; no Flava Flav's or Freeky Tah's to provide the necessary excitement. Rumors had it that your mama went to one but this was never proven. The phenomenon known as the Jones home just wasn't getting any shine.

As years went on MoFo's influence grew to stupendiful proportions and yet the home of Reverend MoFo Jones remained empty. Just as things began to look bleaker than Memphis an unexpected flash of ingenuity, laziness and potential appeared to create the ultimate synthesis to this great MothaFlubba known as Reverend MoFo Jones. A generation of winners and losers, children of the 70s and 80s babies embraced the reverend like no other.

It was late in the game but, I eventually met MoFo Jones. Immediately upon our introduction it was insisted that a visit to the home was necessary. This jerk of a reverend took me home. The Mutafickah presented to me some of the most unsightly and heinous images known to man, woman, child or mutant. Truth tellers became the biggest lying MultiFlickers. Heroes became villainous MuckaFuthas, the ugliest illustrations suddenly pretty MamaFukus, even MCs were turning into sing songy MicahFlutters. There were MoFos everywhere. This home was a hot mess. I was in the presence of greatness redefined. In the blink of an eye, I was hunted, captured and killed close to 200 times.

It is now my duty to aid in protecting the past, present and future from the ill, the bad and the funky. A bold statement of humble and selfish proportions will be made. I will share the secrets that you already know and reveal the ideas you're already interested in. Let's get to Jonesin about ourselves.

I will be your guide through the home of Reverend MoFo Jones.

-j/d

THERE ARE BAD MOFO'S
AND THEN THERE ARE BAD MOFO'S.
WHICH MOFO ARE YOU?

Mofo Jones is

...Divine and Devilish
...Superfly
...Trill
...subject to arrest
...bald in all the wrong places
...that reverend that told you to vote for George Bush
...a legend
...a refugee
...ashy right about now
...a lover and a fighter
...an artistic dynamo
...a 5 time bronze medalist
...a Black Greek from Mykonos
...an illegal alien from Mars
...watching Friday
...a war monger and peace giver
...selling pashminas at the slick price of 2 for $13
...recovering from Blackberry related injuries
...a vegan that drinks Mint Julips and Vitamin Water
to rehydrate from making sweet love
to the sun
...that shady friend who will always have your back
...part of America's best dance crew
...too legit to spit
...as nasty as they wanna be
...a vagabond
...losing his natural mind
...The Head Negro in Charge
...is your baby's mama drama
...extremely weirded out by a pregnant man

...a terrorist to one side and freedom fighter to the other
...a multi millionaire who goes home to the east side trailers
...undefeated at rock, paper, scissors
...still tryin to beat Double Dragon 3
...a social misfit
... a fan of Arsenal FC
...Shani Davis
...Bill Lester
...Mr. Boo L. Yuse
...J*Davey
...Blu & Exile
...Big Baby Jesus
...Bad News Brown
...Deelishis
...Wendy Williams
...Danny Glover
...Too Short
... a Baad Ass Poet
...Melvin Van Peebles
...Nasir, James Earl, Cleopatra, Quincy, Sharon, Serius, Marion, Jim, Kidada, Leroi, Hettie, Edward P, Star, Mike, Norah, Cullen, Pacman, Choloe,Damon, Diana, Clark, and Maela
...the reason we do what we do and
...alive on arrival
... the truth and nothing but the truth
...me
...every last one of you M*****F*****'s

Mofo Jones

...hasn't picked up his pants in about 3 years
...checks out girls then looks to see if anyone caught
him looking
...goes on great dates and has bad sex
...reads Vibe, Vanity Fair and Vogue
... watches All Dat Azz videos
...has trouble spelling Thelonious and pronouncing
Akinyele
...cuts off her dreads for the work place
...dropped out of a doctoral program
...speaks Politics Incorrectly
...needs 20 D Energizers
...knocked out Mike Tyson in 1999
...has been to Iraq on the way to Tibet with a ten year
layover in Sudan
...takes shoes off for no airline
...never took steroids but did get bigger last year
...recites Chappelle Show quotes in her sleep
...wears underwear with dickholes in em
...asked for the deep fade with the part
...has dreams about nightmares from 666years ago
...has been homeless
...plays XBOX online in an effort to remain relevant
...secretly tried to holla at your sister and brother
...hangs with all the Chads from Florida
...sat too close to books and now needs glasses to
watch television
...doesn't believe in Business days
...doesn't have a credit card to purchase online gift
cards
...has body image issues
...was a member of Jack and Jill

...dances better than MC Hammer
...never had enough water in the Slip and Slide
...masturbates to Vanessa Del Rio and Scarface
...washes panties by hand and tongue
...uses PSAT words on Hump Day
...calls others aberrant on Wednesdays
...goes down on up escalators
...was hot for Al B. Sure
...wishes that Denise had graduated from Hillman
...eats Ribs with her hands
...eats grilled octopus with waffles
...got finished off that Hen Rock
...almost died from drinking the big bottle of
Strawberry Cisco
...never wanted the abortion
..gets massive brain freezes from the red white and
blue ice pop
...wants your husband
....speaks 6 dialects of Ebonics
...has 5 million views and 2 million friends
...danced atop the car before the verdict was revealed
...watches Avatar on the low
...still tries the Kid and Play dance from time to time
...doesn't know where to go next
...mentally immigrated to a third world country
...deconstructs culture, lifestyle and twinkies
...eyes the world record in the steeplechase
...looks into the mirror and sees you
...is nothing without you

Who is
The Reverend MoFo Jones?

I am a legend.
Was born and will die as such.
I will fight for us.

Who is The Reverend MoFo Jones?

You think they would lynch
Tiger Woods if the clocks were
turned backwards a few?

We are all the same
We all live in one world house.
Dinner is at 6.

Who is The Reverend MoFo Jones?

I've got these WU-TANG
tendencies that cause me to
dropkick enemies.

My age has made me
invisible to people
who think they matter.

Who is The Reverend MoFo Jones?

I'm the first one in
my family to get in
and finish college.

Spike Lee
A visionary
creates magic with the truth.
The right direction.

Who is The Reverend MoFo Jones?

I'm the fourth one in
my family to get in
and finish college.

I used to shoot off
at the mouth, but now I write
words of funk and awe.

Who is The Reverend MoFo Jones?

Everything is at
the palm of my giant hands,
including your life.

Although I grew up,
not for once did I ever
stop reading rainbows.

Who is The Reverend MoFo Jones?

In the July heat
we never had enough cash
for the good ice cream.

It's raining outside
but for some reason I'm the
only one who's wet.

Who is The Reverend MoFo Jones?

This is not my stop,
in fact this is not my flight.
I'll just use my wings.

Are you a hater?
But think it's all good because
it's done on the low.

Who is The Reverend MoFo Jones?

Meet Super Tuesday
So strong with special powers
Young vote. Kryptonite

I stopped holding doors
because for some reason we
stopped moving forward

Who is The Reverend MoFo Jones?

Despite your crazed thoughts,
I am not an animal.
Call me your master.

I believe in the
ONE and ONLY almighty.
He is my savior.

Who is The Reverend MoFo Jones?

Do you cry like I
do because deep down inside
the pain hasn't stopped?

I am not Bigger
but to you I probably
am. What's in a name?

Who is The Reverend MoFo Jones?

That's my word my dude
if these niggas keep testing
me I won't do shit.

I am a 3rd world
souLja and I'm all souL'd out,
singin while it reigns

Who is The Reverend MoFo Jones?

I was tight at Cliff
Huxtable for the longest.
Cosby went too far.

Sometimes I still think
that September 11th
was an inside job.

Who is The Reverend MoFo Jones?

I'd never heard of
weapons of mass destruction.
vocab malfunction

Mike Tyson
Intimidation,
was it a trip or were you
pushed when the fall came?

Who is The Reverend MoFo Jones?

I probably got
this job cus I was black, part
of me does not care.

Ebonics or jive?
I'm biologically wired
to have my language

Who is The Reverend MoFo Jones?

I never had sex
with any of my teachers,
but a boy could dream.

Will we always be
remembered as the ones who
reelected him?

Who is The Reverend MoFo Jones?

Honestly I can't
remember the last time that
I attended church.

I haven't been in
to see a doctor in just
about 15 years.

Who is The Reverend MoFo Jones?

Fuck it I drink, smoke
weed curse and have lots of sex
am I the bad guy?

Where do you think you're going
Reverend Mofo Jones?

The red black and green
spirits still pass through the air
pumping their fists high

**Where do you think you're going
Reverend Mofo Jones?**

My people hold on
tight. Despite the bumpy ride,
we'll survive this trip.

The silhouette of
tomorrow looks type blurry.
Take out the glasses.

**Where do you think you're going
Reverend Mofo Jones?**

Blessed are those who are
willing to travel that far
into the abyss.

These are the moments
that define your life, spirit
and your legacy.

**Where do you think you're going
Reverend Mofo Jones?**

The public schools in
my neighborhood are not good.
How are they in yours?

If we learned how to
tie shoelaces then we can
learn to fight for peace.

**Where do you think you're going
Reverend Mofo Jones?**

We once scrapped with our
hands then a kid brought a knife
now the bullets fight.

I'll leave a voicemail
with hope that the ancestors
will shoot me a text.

**Where do you think you're going
Reverend Mofo Jones?**

Change is everywhere.
Sometimes all it takes is to
read from right to left

What the fuck do I
care about revolutions?
I need that paper.

**Where do you think you're going
Reverend Mofo Jones?**

Ol Massa doesn't
look the same but don't worry
we are still enslaved.

In 1804
they decided that they had
enough. So now what?

**Where do you think you're going
Reverend Mofo Jones?**

A new leader will
emerge the moment you look
into a mirror.

There was a shooting.
There was a point where tears flowed.
Now we are immune.

**Where do you think you're going
Reverend Mofo Jones?**

I've opened my eyes
only to find myself trapped
in a great trick bag.

One of these days the
vessel will start to go down.
Will you sink or swim?

**Where do you think you're going
Reverend Mofo Jones?**

Our words could be the
ones that spark the mother of
all revolutions.

Where's Waldo? He's at
the liquor store bodega
fried chicken gun shop.

**Where do you think you're going
Reverend Mofo Jones?**

Running in circles
without the proper track shoes
more hurdles to face

My freedom has been
delayed because my shoes have
been deemed suspicious

**Where do you think you're going
Reverend Mofo Jones?**

Every time I look
and everywhere I go there
is a funky smell.

What are you listening to MoFo Jones?

The soundtrack of my
life makes ears bleed like they have
never bled before

What are you listening to MoFo Jones?

When did Flava Flav
become people's enemy
number one one one?

Hey! Have you seen rap?
If so please holla at me.
My elements drowned.

What are you listening to MoFo Jones?

And my vote goes to
Andre 3000 as the
funkiest MC.

The voice of freedom
is getting muffled by the
excess background noise.

What are you listening to MoFo Jones?

They shout blasphemy
just cus I called you out gard.
The battle's still on!

Do you consider
me to be less black because
I like Dave Matthews?

What are you listening to MoFo Jones?

Tron
America does
not want to see us work. They
want to see us live!

I am the MC
and you shall be the DJ.
Together we reign!

What are you listening to MoFo Jones?

Nas
Represent because
any day could be our last
days in the jungle

Biggie
stereotype of
a black man misunderstood
but it's still all good

What are you listening to MoFo Jones?

I will not carry
hip hop's coffin on this day.
I think it's empty.

Boom bap scientists
create earthquakes with their sick
instruments of fresh.

What are you listening to MoFo Jones?

Do you remember
taping Canibus freestyles
from the radio?

My music has been
co-opted by something quite
forceful and ugly.

What are you listening to MoFo Jones?

Kanye
Who the kids gonna
listen to? Huh! I guess me
if it isn't you.

Who says hip hop is
dead cus if that beat is hot
I'm alive and well

What are you listening to MoFo Jones?

Cats singing off key
will never unlock the truth
about my hip hop.

Little Brother
Like I could stick you
up with a knife. Like I could
rape you with a verse...

What are you listening to MoFo Jones?

Do you hear voices?
If so what are they telling
you? Mine say freedom.

Jay-Z
Homie, respect the
game that should be it. What you
eat don't make me shit

What are you listening to MoFo Jones?

This is bigger than
the both of us combined let's.
lower the volume.

If you keep talking
then we won't be able to
hear the youngins cry.

What are you listening to MoFo Jones?

The only super
sweet 16 I know involves
a mic and some bars.

I'm looking for a
rapping antibiotic
to cure the bullshit.

What are you listening to MoFo Jones?

Lauryn
When I took deep breaths
I was inhaling bliss. I
miss education.

Who loves the Reverend Mofo Jones?

I will hold your hand
because I know what it feels
like to have fallen.

Who loves the Reverend Mofo Jones?

If I had known you
were gonna treat me this way,
I woulda been left.

Where in the world is
Carmen Sandiego and
has she seen my dad?

Who loves the Reverend Mofo Jones?

and now playing the
part of your mother and your
father, it is me

my love will make you
cry cringe cheer and cha cha slide
across all bayous

Who loves the Reverend Mofo Jones?

Is your partner a
black woman? Yes. But aren't you
also a woman.

Never again will
I be afraid to say this
out loud. I love you!

Who loves the Reverend Mofo Jones?

To think our peoples
said that we would never last
yet we took that chance

May I taste your tears
of joy to quench the thirst for
love and paradise

Who loves the Reverend Mofo Jones?

we don't need the vote
of congress to define the
strength of this union

She hesitated
before making that final
phone call to dead it.

Who loves the Reverend Mofo Jones?

Immaturity
has just cost me another
good relationship.

As the misery
grows, pain plays at high octaves.
My love stays supreme

Who loves the Reverend Mofo Jones?

My body yearns to
be with your body and thus
united we love

Don't front as if you
care about me, we both know
this is just a beat

Who loves the Reverend Mofo Jones?

I am afraid to
hold your hand because you have
let it go before.

Let me hold your breath
and I promise you that it
will be deeply loved.

Who loves the Reverend Mofo Jones?

underneath the clouds
and standing there drenched in sweat
your beauty scares me

My homeboy Widley
wears his heart on his short sleeve
so fashionably

Who loves the Reverend Mofo Jones?

Your game is way too
slick for me. Therefore I am
choosing to fall back

I should've never
played her cus now that she's gone
I can only dream.

Who loves the Reverend Mofo Jones?

You are making my
heart hop, skip and jump to some
double dutch rhythms.

The dog and jumpoff
quit their ways and lived a nice
slow life together.

Who loves the Reverend Mofo Jones?

Brothers, don't be so
scared of the union between
your other brothers.

There are no brothers
out there because they just don't
dig fine black women.

Who loves the Reverend Mofo Jones?

I am your single
father. Don't worry you will
never be alone

What are you doing Reverend Mofo Jones?

I salute a flag
that cheerleaders once waved to
celebrate my death.

What are you doing Reverend Mofo Jones?

In two thousand 4
I voted and died. In two
thousand 8, I changed.

read all the faces
see the hidden become truth
feed me Mini feed

What are you doing Reverend Mofo Jones?

Am I spending too
much time on the Internet?
Let me google that.

I took a chance by
having unprotected sex
with someone unknown.

What are you doing Reverend Mofo Jones?

Why do I need to
take care of my children? The
TV can do that.

Project terrorists
are armed with rocks and ready
to smoke something up.

What are you doing Reverend Mofo Jones?

How much do you think
it would cost to super size
my body and soul?

Did you pay the rent?
No. I just bought an Iphone.
So you played the rent.

What are you doing Reverend Mofo Jones?

It seems that I have
broken my thumb in a freak
texting accident.

I have been baptized
by a hurricane praying,
for swimming lessons

What are you doing Reverend Mofo Jones?

After the sermon
my pockets felt emptier.
And the pastor smiled

Let's say I wrote it.
If I killed it, would you read
it? I'm not guilty.

What are you doing Reverend Mofo Jones?

Hey everyone I
just snitched on the ignorance
that is "no snitchin".

Now that I've paid an
arm and leg for these Jordan's,
I'm left with one foot.

What are you doing Reverend Mofo Jones?

I can't believe I
just spent so much money on
some damn vodka cran.

When you are met by
walls don't break the walls down. Mash
up the wall builder.

What are you doing Reverend Mofo Jones?

You don't treat me the
same because I pronounce my
R's different from you.

Did it take long for
you to start singing those R.
Kelly songs again?

What are you doing Reverend Mofo Jones?

Jacko
We all walked on moons
Questionable decisions
Dancing atop cars

At what age are you
too old to have your pants sag
way below your ass?

What are you doing Reverend Mofo Jones?

Who you callin a
bitch? Your mother, Rosa Parks,
Harriet Tubman...

Get bent. No reason.
Drink responsibly for what?
The hurt feels so good.

What are you doing Reverend Mofo Jones?

They thought it was lame,
so they said no protection.
A silent death march.

As of today my
Playstation 3 will be moved
into my top 8.

What are you doing Reverend Mofo Jones?

the reason I can't
find my mom is because she
is locked behind bars

MoFo Jones, can you do me a solid?

It seems to be that
the only children getting
left behind are mine

MoFo Jones, can you do me a solid?

Fight for my country.
When I return home they are
not fighting for me.

Two years after the
levees broke sin city is
still flowin out tears.

MoFo Jones, can you do me a solid?

I've been getting played
for what seems like my whole life
and the hurt still hurts.

Black boy do you read
the fine print that says you are
an ugly person?

MoFo Jones, can you do me a solid?

Lolita and her
little homie Shaniqua
are in some trouble.

white masks while light out
behind close doors black faces
frontin to maintain

MoFo Jones, can you do me a solid?

If you loosen these
handcuffs I promise to lift
every voice and sing.

I'm in this jail cell
and not in 5th period
cus my poor hurt bad

MoFo Jones, can you do me a solid?

Do the leaders of
the civil rights movement still
sacrifice for us?

don't get it twisted
we are involved in a fight
time to buckle down

MoFo Jones, can you do me a solid?

I have cocoa bread
dreams on rainy days each time
hoping for less beef.

rather than helping
my sister and brother with
their drug problem. JAIL.

MoFo Jones, can you do me a solid?

Taking some time to
slow down and think never hurts
the community.

Make up your mind fam.
in the house or on the field
collecting the check

MoFo Jones, can you do me a solid?

The person in charge
of telling my life story
has trouble reading.

I read an Email
that said black people don't read.
Let's escape that lie.

MoFo Jones, can you do me a solid?

It hurts to watch them
stand defenseless against a
war on their young souls.

little boys failing
every single class are in
search of some guidance

MoFo Jones, can you do me a solid?

I've never read Black
Boy, Invisible Man or
the Souls of Black Folk.

In Kenya 7
hundred folks die everyday
from HIV/AIDS

MoFo Jones, can you do me a solid?

What's more important
Brad Pitt and Angelina
or a free Tibet?

That hurricane shed
some light on the fact that I
was already poor.

MoFo Jones, can you do me a solid?

mayonnaise sandwich
and sugar water for lunch
and sometimes dinner

I've been fishing now
for some months and the jobs just
are not biting back

MoFo Jones, can you do me a solid?

I can't afford gas.
I cant afford insurance
Why am I driving?

What's really good MoFo Jones?

Little Wayne makes more
money than the woman who
taught me how to read.

What's really good MoFo Jones?

They care more about
a Barry Bonds drug habit
then war in Iraq.

Stop acting like shit
is all good while this white dude
keeps saying nigga.

What's really good MoFo Jones?

Stop acting like shit
is all good while this black dude
keeps saying nigga.

There is a recall
on white Jesus pieces for
miracle failure.

What's really good MoFo Jones?

With fresh lashings on
my back I continue to
dunk these basketballs.

This Nigger was freed.
That Nigga is wildin out.
Wait, what just happened?

What's really good MoFo Jones?

I woke up early,
Only to find myself trapped
in a foreign place

My rich is richer
than your rich because I have
more jails in my town.

What's really good MoFo Jones?

Is Sean Bell now dead
because some cops lost control?
Still doesn't make sense.

Where do the kids keep
getting all these fucking guns
and why do they shoot?

What's really good MoFo Jones?

McDonald's.Starbucks
FBI. CIA. FOX
FCC the Klan?

the white smoke has cleared
beyond the mountains. Beauty
too high to notice.

What's really good MoFo Jones?

I took this acne
medicine and it gave me
some high blood pressure

Bill Clinton is black
but Barack ain't black enough.
What is going on?

What's really good MoFo Jones?

When I watch the news
I see painful images
of propaganda

Hey Knickerbocker
What are your priorities?
Money. Cash. Ho's. Son!

What's really good MoFo Jones?

Let me get this straight,
it's gonna cost how much for
this yearly checkup?

so I have this cut,
but I can't find a band-aid
to match my skin tone

What's really good MoFo Jones?

Please call customer
service. Para Espanol
oprima cinco.

I pledge allegiance
to the United States of
the great Queen Oprah.

What's really good MoFo Jones?

Black men fair as well
as a white felon in terms
of finding a job.

We are Reverend MoFo Jones!

Johnette Ellis
ignorance of the
masses has taught me that i
know. shit. elite. bitch?

We are Reverend MoFo Jones !

Alexandros Orphanides
captain of the ship
never master of the seas
ocean - destiny

Anthony Samuels
Sleeping Men Dream, Then
Awake To Reality
Then Realizing Life's Ills

We are Reverend MoFo Jones !

Nicol Corsey
The dark cavities
cowering away from light
dismantling souls.

Brad Smith
Vick murders a dog.
The cops murder a nigger.
who ends up in jail?

We are Reverend MoFo Jones !

Denmark Baraka
I have always been
going green its just that mine
was another shade

Laurence Bass
I love to love you.
You ask me when will we wed.
I have no real clue.

We are Reverend MoFo Jones !

Jessica Nabongo
I want the world and
if you don't give it to me
somebody else will

Johnette Ellis
behind my ears are
words never meant to be heard,
can't speak in language.

We are Reverend MoFo Jones !

Laurence Bass
Hipsters make me sick.
You look like a goddamn fool!
Invention is dead.

SoSoon
Hip Hop is an art
Real art reflects our real lives
Hip Hop equals life

We are Reverend MoFo Jones !

Jasmine Grant
We're lost in the hype
Can you hear our voices cry
over bass and snares

Nafeesah Allen
shadows fall on leaves
and they onto the pavement
this city of lights

We are Reverend MoFo Jones !

Kyle Ishmael
Born of the dreamers
Alone not lonely in the
heaven of our dreams

Jessica Nabongo
i cried so much that
i don't have anymore tears
i am over you.

We are Reverend MoFo Jones !

James Oluwole Adeyomoye
How many friends will
we continue losing when
we cannot live free

R. Holland
I'm Black born in a
white society it's the
system or the game

We are Reverend MoFo Jones !

Amari Chris Johnson
i couldn't speak my
heart's words through my throat because
the rope was too tight

Brooke Harris
let's walk hand in hand
trim, red-brown skin, and lovely
you're my trophy man

We are Reverend MoFo Jones !

Amari Chris Johnson
Mad sisters screaming
Africa all in they walk.
God stay showing off.

Acknowledgements

To the lovely lady who called me a whack MoFo
with utmost negative vibes in her soul and to the
brother who on the same day called me a bad
MoFo with the goodness in his heart. You were
both inspirations.

Shout out Linnette, Megan, Lemu, Johnie,
Castina and to all my dear brothers and sisters
who were the ultimate guides during the early
stages of this process, your critique, responses
and beautiful ideas helped in my discovery and
understanding of this home.

Thank You for your Words,
James Oluwole Adeyomoye, Nafeesah Allen,
Denmark Baraka, Laurence Bass, Nicole Corsey
R. Holland, Kyle Ishmael, Johnette Ellis, Jasmine
Grant, Brooke Harris, Amari Chris Johnson,
Jessica Nabongo Alexandros Orphanides,
Anthony Samuels, SoSoon and Brad Smith

Joe Gilpin Jr., for your excellent back cover
design. Once again you've outdone yourself.

Peace.Love.Funk
And I'm out this Muthafucka!!
j/d

A NOTE ABOUT THE AUTHOR

Jeffrey Dessources is a writer and emcee of Haitian descent. He received his M.A. in English Literature from St. John's University and is the author of the text *do not hold doors.* He currently works and teaches at the College of Mount Saint Vincent.

grew bap has arrived.